CLOSE TO THE UNDERTOW

Poems on the experience of ministry

by BONNIE L. BAIRD

CLOSE TO THE UNDERTOW

ISBN 978-0-9940973-7-8 (print book)

ISBN 978-0-9940973-1-6 (electronic book)

Select titles also by Bonnie L. Baird

Poetry

Walk Me To The Door, Love:

Notes Written to the Beloved in the First Two Years of Grief

I Smell Stars:

Final Twelve Years of a Marriage

Lightning Strikes:

Reflections on Complicated Family Relationships

Songs in the Night:

Poems for Use in the Church and of Lamentation

Prose

Survival of the Dangly Green Parrot Earrings

CD

Walk Me To The Door, Love

I Smell Stars

This book is dedicated to all who work in the fields of the Lord.

ACKNOWLEDGEMENTS

Thank you to my friend Laurie Omstead, clergy colleague, friend and patient listener of my poetry over the years, and to Heather Veinotte, writer, friend and writing mentor.

My thanks as well to Frauke Spanuth of Croco Designs for her vibrant and creative cover art and interior design of this book.

CONTENTS

Into Your Hands

〰

Into
these hands
cupped

    tiny   massive
      and   and
        smooth   firm
          and   and
            calloused   trembling
              and   and
           gnarled

and scarred

into this cup expectant
I
place
pieces of You
pieces of me

Ministry and Matters of the Heart

This is delicate work
no doubt about it

some ego there needs to be else you would never attempt it
too much and everything goes sideways

and you can consult the more experienced in your field all you want
but ultimately it's up to you
how much pressure to apply
what to leave in, cut out
bypass, reconnect
create

do no damage
is a good guideline but most of the time there is some
it's not exact, this work
and the more tired you get the riskier it is for everyone

what healing there can be
depends on so much more than what you bring to the table
don't forget that: ultimately it's out of your hands

this is delicate work
no doubt about it

OFFERINGS

I buried
a little girl this week
over her ashes said
words of blessing
I say to children at the altar rail Sunday mornings

she is so little
this woman
drinks half her daily calories in triple creamed tea we bring her
all week she keeps watch
over the bed on which her partner
slips gradually into
oblivion
Am I making the right decision? she asks as doctors
remove her options one by one

I don't know why my wife won't go to church anymore
the old man says (we talk about such things
he likes things orderly, explained)
You go for the sacraments
but mainly you go for community....I used to take up collection, you know
you'd be surprised what people put on the plate

fragments of the week

so much in common we have
unacknowledged
except by such as us who look
over the offerings
(you'd be surprised what people have on their plate)
pronounce them Blessed

Ash Wednesday Service
in the Dark

The altar
is the only lit spot
in this dark vaulted space

power out all around us in the howling wind
yet here we sit

ready to acknowledge how frail we really are
Dust you are...
ready to admit some of us won't be here next year
and will return to...

bearing crosses no one can see
save for those on our foreheads

finite and infinite
radiance and darkness

O Blender of Opposites,
hold us in this moment close
mark us as yours

COMMITTAL

The hole is narrow and deep
and the box
sits in it
gathering up the rain about us
gathering in the roses grandchildren brought

after the collared words are said
and the circle of family/friends eases out
you wait
umbrellaed and alone
on the edge
for someone to come
fill it in

Committal Maundy Thursday

We renew old vows
bring our jars ready to be filled again with holy oil

Lord, fill us as these jars
to overflowing when the holes are deep and narrow
and the rain slants in

keep us from drowning
in all but you

AFTER 54 YEARS OF MARRIAGE

What I notice
isn't the oblong box before us
the cross of sand melting away
mud seeping into our shoes
flowers gingerly set at odd angles

I notice the suit pants
extending beyond the protective scope of umbrella
beautiful
lightweight
woolen suit pants
like those he might have worn at his wedding,
wheeling
round a decorated room with his lady on his arm…
how they could dance then!
his legs at right angles now to the ground
folded neatly between the wheels
of his chair
a dark stain growing in the rain

FRAGMENTS

We cluster
a distance from the scene

not close enough to interfere

but close
he's still inside

and we will wait however long it takes

everything's muted, reflectant in this cold wet place
lights, the report ricocheting
about us

as the mist moves in past boat and traps
and the men move out
carrying his weight between them
one looks down, stoops, picks up something white from the grass

got to keep it together

FISHING BOAT AFTER THE FUNERAL

After it is over
he tows the empty shell to a friend's place

lays the layers down
one by one, fiber on fiber, with his big fisherman's hands
building the guts from the inside out
a few hatches open you have to be wary of
walking around on the deck

he names it My Brother's Wish, his own now
that the others have passed on,
laid down and sealed up tight

on a fine fall day
slips into bay waters
back end wide open for traps

DEPOSIT FOR THE REV

You deposit your message on the office phone
towards the end of the day

coiled and
rising
toward anyone
who answers

the energy it takes...

And somewhere this night
an old man
lies on a hospital bed slowly losing the memory of who he is
a woman remembers when she had
two breasts
Christmas is being planned without a four-year-old
who lies
freshly buried under snow in the churchyard

Appalled at baptismal practices in the church and at my attitude
in particular
you will be taking your grandson
and family
somewhere else

some place where they really care

NOAH?

Noah?
was this what it felt like?
no one seeing the rains coming
only the lunacy of building in a dry place
without a whole lot of help

timber by timber
watching emptiness convert into something you can hold the world within
knowing you have never seen such a thing before but building anyway
for the rains coming
and the door shutting
and everything solid save this slipping away

Your Leaving

The news of your leaving
catches everyone by surprise

we thought your ticket was for a later date

we had intended to visit
catch up on missed conversations
ask your opinion on some important and not so important matters
thank you for being Present

It is first light and you are gone
we thought we had longer

for Darlene on her D. day

GETHSEMANE

She kneels in Gethsemane
each time she stands beside the washer
and loads another shirt

and she has loved him sixty years or more

she changes the dressings and loads the shirts
that won't stay dry from the weeping of his wound
and in the quiet of the basement

she prays for him to stay
she prays for him to go
she prays for the strength to see him home

BULLIES BY ANY OTHER NAME

Speak softly and carry a big stick
a president long ago counselled

but he wasn't talking about you
cane in hand hobbling to your seat

the group's assembling and you,
before most of them came,
have already expressed your opinion
your disappointment
in a take-no-prisoners way
The agenda isn't what you expected
Didn't we make it clear?
It will be a lecture, not a listening
You know a lecture when you hear it
and you for one will not sit through it
You are out of here as soon as you can get your cane
under you, steady yourself.

I must admit I am relieved
it will be difficult enough this time
without **you**

and yet you stay
add a comment here and there
tempered now in the presence of others
at the end of the meeting
smile
thank me for coming
wave to me from your car

but you set the tone, didn't you?
a heads-up to what was coming
a practice run at keeping my temper

a bully by any other name

PERSONALLY

One piece of advice, our guest speaker says:
whatever you do
don't take it personally

it's clergy quiet day and we've gathered
hoping for a word or two
distilled into something we can use
in the trenches

when things get muddy and shots are fired
and toxicity drifts toward us

when the meeting's called and you're sitting up front
as resignations
land on the table
one
by
one
when the church sits divided
and your word, the one you earn your living by, is questioned
by the powers that be
who weren't there when what happened
happened
don't take it personally

when the finger's pointing in your face and the blood's rising
and the forum is public
don't take it personally

when you're told by your superior
to go after the ones that tore you and the others apart

for that's what a real pastor does
and they're hurting too, don't you know
and if you won't go
perhaps another clergy will on your behalf
don't take it personally
it's not about you

don't take it personally

Why the hell not?

What the Psychiatrist Told the Clergy About Anger

Spike twenty points
and you're into primal territory

walk away, walk away

spike twenty points
and the blood's rushing looking for a way out
what a bloody mess

walk away, walk away

spike twenty points
in a heartbeat breath's changing
that fast and all you are and care to be
is gone
who's responsible won't matter

walk away, walk away
Run

Postcard One: Let Me Hear of Your Steadfast Love

Let me hear of your steadfast love in the morning from Psalm 143

At first, the thought of telling his mom had made his head swim. She had wanted so much more for him. Soon everyone was commenting, even strangers. Strange thing was, he felt ready now to be a father. Maybe it was in the genes. His mom had been young with him, maybe even younger, and she had managed. She was young still though the fast-moving cancer had stolen much.

The thought of telling her had made his head swim but that was another time ages ago.

Now, in the first light of morning, he watches her cradle his brand new son. Touch his feet, his hands. "Just like you," she says, "just like you."

Postcard Two: Even The Sparrow

*Even the sparrow finds a home, and the swallow a nest for
herself, where she may lay her young at your altars, O Lord.*
from Psalm 84

She fashioned a tiny bird's nest out of the hair she found each morning in
the sink. It didn't surprise her that none of her children wanted it. It was bad
enough knowing she was losing her hair to the treatments without this tiny
reminder. But she liked it. It appealed to her sense of everything being useful,
recycled. It also struck her as funny, people's reactions to it and to her hairless
head.

Sometimes as she slipped into sleep, she felt her hair flowing about her…long
and luxurious now, flowing about her knees and upon the wind, beckoning
into its branches…safe refuge, safe refuge for all her children.

On Retreat

We arrive carrying overstuffed bags, schedules, minds
energy leaked out
somewhere along the way
****

in little corners
recreate the familiar
set out books shelved for months
locate room numbers of friends
unpack
****

Sister Rose, you welcome us into your home
set a fine table: pancakes, porridge, fruit
tuck extra blankets, pillows into our spaces
cookies, milk on the sideboard
reminds me of something long ago when my son was young…
ah, yes:
daycare for clergy
****

sixteen clergy
new and old
newly minted old ones too
school, former careers, supervisors, neighbouring workplaces, friends
so many connections

evensong begins
the many begin to blend
as we turn towards the Other
in whose service we are

****

can it be morning already
and what on earth am I doing here
singing morning prayer
first light?
and is this why the first birds I hear early morning
are usually crows?

****

six meditations and one could long for more
stories linking heart and mind
not a sound in this room
of vocal people
but the conductor's voice
concentration

****

quiet
hovers
among us
like a note struck of crystal

****

tonight I sit in my room
preferring a book to compline
the floor filtering the prayers, the singing
voices rising like incense to the Lord and me

****

someone spent 45 minutes ·
in the shower this morning
someone else prayed for the state of his soul
and a little hot water

****

time to go
no one breaks the silence at breakfast

though now we may
we are not ready yet to share location

newly turned soil for the moment
open again to the air, light
winged visitors

NOTHING MAKES SENSE

On the brink of choosing the coffin
she stamps her feet and just holds on to one long NOOOOO
and nothing makes sense
not being here or meeting with me
or picking out flowers or deciding, deciding, deciding
and nothing makes sense
and how can he just not
Be
and can we use this prayer book another priest gave them
on their wedding day
for his funeral:
there is a kind of symmetry
and nothing makes sense
nothing makes sense
this nothing

BOUNDARIES

Somewhere I've stepped across the thin border
separating
former rector from current
priest from friend

your firm and rather courteous response the only clue

no detonations
barbed wire wounds to cope with

still…

these places need to be better posted

COLLEGIALITY

After the dissection
we identify the parts with labels that go on easier
than they come off

something always
remains:
stickiness
piece of label
jagged edge where it once was

Bubbles

I sit with "my" people in a room full of circles
each round table discussion
focused on local circumstance

there
a former rector watches familiar faces around me
animate with delight, concentration
there
another sits with the home team
which lifted me up and led me here
while
I watch someone competent but not me
at table with people I served once

beloved people of past lives

circles almost touching circles...
everything in its season...
the spaces between so small but there...
bubbles rising in a glass

SORTING IT OUT ON MOVING DAY

We've been measuring and some key pieces will have to go
we've lugged around for years
grown accustomed to…

the put-anything-out-by-the-curb day is almost upon us
and who's to say what is junk?
meaningful?
or just excess?

there will be some nosing through what we leave behind
it's to be expected

this is harder than I thought

FOR LITTLE SAMUEL:
SIX WEEKS EARLY

You are perfect
miniature of all you will be

one long fingered hand laid on your breast
in gentle blessing
as you acknowledge a familiar voice
slight turn of head towards us
in your cubed off space

That one so little
could bear such message
fingers formed so newly connect so firmly
so many intertwine

that even I who had considered
not living my calling anymore
should pause
before your glory,
remember how to pray

This Body the Church

This body—your body, my body—
to which we belong
is not our body

we are only a part
of the whole which cannot live apart
from the One who calls us into being

we are flawed
scarred and scared and sacred
unrecognizable at times even to ourselves
and what we have done and left undone in the past
affects us now
this body

we are beautiful
made in his image
imagining a world different: just and compassionate,
enough for everyone and
everyone enough in themselves
reaching out with all our being to make it so

we cannot see ourselves from a distance
cannot know the difference we make really
we cannot heal ourselves or remove these scars

though there is One who can and does over and over again
convicting, absolving
touching, making whole
pouring out and breaking for us
pieces of himself given to this body

imperfect

this body to which we belong
is not our body

About the Author

Bonnie Baird is a writer, Anglican priest, and blessed mom and grandma currently living along Nova Scotia's South Shore.

www.ingramcontent.com/pod-product-compliance
Lightning Source LLC
LaVergne TN
LVHW090047090426
835511LV00031B/512